FLYING CARS

and Other Transportation Tech

World Book, Inc.
180 North LaSalle Street
Suite 900
Chicago, Illinois 60601
USA

For information about other "Cool Tech" titles, as well as other World Book print and digital publications, please go to www.worldbook.com.

For information about other World Book publications, call 1-800-WORLDBK (967-5325).

For information about sales to schools and libraries, call 1-800-975-3250 (United States) or 1-800-837-5365 (Canada).

Library of Congress Cataloging-in-Publication Data for this volume has been applied for.

Cool Tech
ISBN: 978-0-7166-2429-5 (set, hc.)

Flying Cars and Other Transportation Tech
ISBN: 978-0-7166-2430-1 (hc.)

Also available as:
ISBN: 978-0-7166-2447-9 (e-book)

Printed in China by RR Donnelley,
Guangdong Province
1st printing July 2019

STAFF

Editorial

Writer
William D. Adams

Manager, New Content
Jeff De La Rosa

Manager, New Product
Development
Nick Kilzer

Proofreader
Nathalie Strassheim

Manager, Contracts and
Compliance
(Rights and Permissions)
Loranne K. Shields

Manager, Indexing Services
David Pofelski

Digital

Director, Digital Product
Development
Erika Meller

Digital Product Manager
Jonathan Wills

Graphics and Design

Senior Designer
Don DiSante

Media Editor
Rosalia Bledsoe

Manufacturing/
Production

Manufacturing Manager
Anne Fritzinger

Production Specialist
Curley Hunter

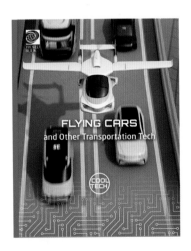

Credit: © Chesky/Shutterstock

CONTENTS

INTRODUCTION

Imagine you want to visit a friend over the weekend, but your friend lives in the next big city over. It's too close to fly. On Saturday morning, you walk out of your house to the car waiting for you at the curb. You read the morning news as it quietly drives you to a small regional airport. You board a helicopter-like pod and wait a few minutes as more passengers arrive. Then, you're off! You rise into the sky, enjoying the breathtaking views of the city below. The pod touches down on the roof of a transit station. You go downstairs, check in, and board what looks like a small airplane **fuselage.** It leaves the station and speeds through a tube at hundreds of miles or kilometers per hour. You've made it to your friend's city in time for brunch—without any of the flying or driving being done by a person! That might sound like science fiction, but all of these technologies are already being developed.

Transportation is the fabric that binds society together. It's how workers get to their jobs, shoppers get to stores, and vacationers get to their destinations. It's also how goods and materials get to factories, worksites, and stores. Because just about everything—and everyone—uses transportation, improvements to transportation can have huge impacts on our lives. In the last 100 years, the automobile has changed how people get around and how cities are designed. In the last 50 years, jet-powered airplanes have taken people around the globe. Technologies being developed today could change the world in a similar way in the next 50 years.

What are some of the next big things on the horizon in the field of transportation? What changes will these advancements bring about? How will you get where you need to go in the future? Read on to learn more about the future—and history—of transportation!

1 FLYING CARS

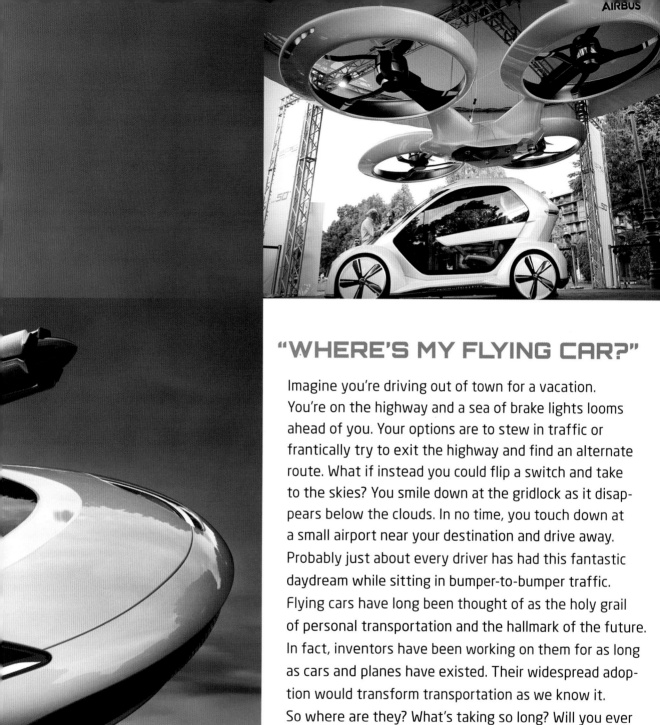

"WHERE'S MY FLYING CAR?"

Imagine you're driving out of town for a vacation. You're on the highway and a sea of brake lights looms ahead of you. Your options are to stew in traffic or frantically try to exit the highway and find an alternate route. What if instead you could flip a switch and take to the skies? You smile down at the gridlock as it disappears below the clouds. In no time, you touch down at a small airport near your destination and drive away. Probably just about every driver has had this fantastic daydream while sitting in bumper-to-bumper traffic. Flying cars have long been thought of as the holy grail of personal transportation and the hallmark of the future. In fact, inventors have been working on them for as long as cars and planes have existed. Their widespread adoption would transform transportation as we know it. So where are they? What's taking so long? Will you ever be able to soar unencumbered over traffic?

ENGINEERING CHALLENGE: JACK OF ALL TRADES, MASTER OF NONE

Inventors created cars and airplanes at about the same time, around 1900. Many people thought it was only a matter of time before the two merged into one universal mode of transportation. It seemed to be the logical extension of the freedom of driving. It also made sense from a design perspective. Early cars and airplanes faced some of the same challenges: the need for a sturdy frame, reliable controls, and a powerful but lightweight engine.

But as both auto and air travel got faster and more complex, their engineering requirements split. A car is more likely to be involved in an accident, so it needs to be able to protect its driver and passengers. In aircraft, efficiency is king. An aircraft needs to be as light as possible to reduce the amount of fuel it uses. Designers of modern flying cars must find a way to successfully balance safety and

Modern flying car designs dispense with clunky wings to generate lift. Instead, compact, folding wings and **ducted propellers** get them airborne.

Early flying car designs struggled with the problem of where to put the wings when driving on the road. Most attempts to solve this problem were less than ideal.

efficiency. Almost every design decision made to improve one compromises the other. And workarounds are expensive.

Another engineering challenge has hindered the development of the flying car: where do the wings go? Most aircraft use wings to generate **lift** for flight. But when driving, wings could cause a flying car to take flight at the wrong times! Wings also take up way too much space on the road. Therefore, designers of flying cars have to figure out what to do with the craft's wings when it's driving. In some designs, the wings detach and are left behind. In others, such as the Taylor Aerocar of the 1950's pictured above, the wings were removed and towed behind the vehicle during driving. Still others have the wings and tail fold down into the body of the vehicle. Each design has its own disadvantages.

Some inventors have dispensed with big wings by including ducted propellers or jet engines in their designs. But such devices use large amounts of energy or burn large amounts of fuel, limiting the flying car's range.

LEAVING THE ROAD BEHIND

Should a flying car look more like an airplane or an automobile? Early flying car designs approached the problem by trying to combine the essential elements of both cars and airplanes in a single vehicle. The resulting vehicles could be both driven or flown, but they were some pretty ungainly rides. Modern flying car engineers have begun thinking outside of traditional views of cars and airplanes to create unique compact designs that perform well and look good.

Folding wings. One attempt to solve the problem of bulky wings in flying car designs was to make the wings foldable. Much like a typical convertible, where the roof of the car folds neatly into the trunk, foldable wings can be retracted when the flying car is driving on the road. While such designs do both fly and drive, the bulky wings are ungainly, add weight, and decrease fuel efficiency.

The Autoplane couldn't stay in its lane. Some of the first aviation pioneers were interested in flying cars. American inventor Glenn Curtiss, the first person to receive a U.S. pilot's license, created a flying car called the Autoplane *(above)*. A pilot could drive two passengers at speeds of up to 45 miles per hour and fly up to 65 miles per hour. But the prototype only made short hops and never flew for a sustained period of time. Furthermore, the huge, fixed wings would have been a hazard to other cars.

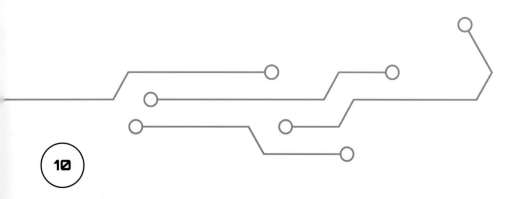

Foldable wings mean this car can transition into an airplane with the push of a button. But newer flying car designs rely less on big wings to take flight.

Ducted propellers. One of the main challenges facing flying cars is how to take off at the slow speed of a driving car. Engineers can solve this problem in flying car designs using ducted propellers. Placing a ring, or duct, around a propeller increases the efficiency and power dramatically. Ducted propellers can generate high thrust necessary for a car to take off at lower engine speeds, with smaller or no wings!

Pilot school. If you own a flying car, do you need a driver's license or a pilot's license? Both! Becoming a pilot requires tests and many hours of training, creating another barrier to widespread adoption of flying cars.

2 SELF-DRIVING CARS

CARS THAT DRIVE THEMSELVES

The average American spends more than 40 hours per year stuck in traffic. That's almost an entire weekend spent yawning, staring out the window, and drumming your fingers on the steering wheel. What if we could do something more fun with that time? What if everyone in the car could be passengers, spending the trip reading, watching television, or talking with friends and family in the car?

Today, dozens of companies are hard at work on the technology to allow cars to drive themselves. Using sophisticated sensors, powerful computers, and artificial intelligence techniques, such self-driving cars could take us where we needed to go without a human taking the wheel.

Even more important, self-driving cars can help save lives! In the United States alone, around 40,000 people are killed each year in vehicle accidents. Most of these accidents were caused by human mistakes. Self-driving cars, on the other hand, never get drunk, fall asleep, or drive distracted. Their use could greatly reduce the number of vehicle injuries and deaths.

PARTS OF A SELF-DRIVING CAR

A modern car is already an extremely complex machine. It's chock-full of motors, gears, and even a number of **sensors** and computers. A self-driving car will require dozens of systems working together to get its passengers safely from one place to another.

GPS. In order to go anywhere, a self-driving car needs to know where it is. Self-driving cars will be equipped with a **Global Positioning System** (GPS).

Lidar. The most important sensor for self-driving cars is **lidar,** which stands for *l*ight *d*etection *a*nd *r*anging. In a lidar unit, dozens of **lasers** send pulses of light into the environment. (The light produced by these lasers is usually a kind people can't see called **infrared rays.**) Some of the light bounces off surfaces in the environment and returns to the lidar unit and is picked up by receivers. The longer the light takes to return, the farther away the surface it bounced off. The car's computer uses this information to create a constantly-updating picture of where it is. A few companies, notably the luxury electric car manufacturer Tesla, are trying to create self-driving cars without lidar to avoid its high costs.

Radar. Radar stands for *r*adio *d*etection *a*nd *r*anging. Radar works the same way lidar does, but it uses radio waves instead of infrared rays. Radio waves have lower frequencies than infrared, so radar can't match lidar's **resolution.** But radar can see through snow and fog. It's also relatively cheap and reliable, having been in use for decades.

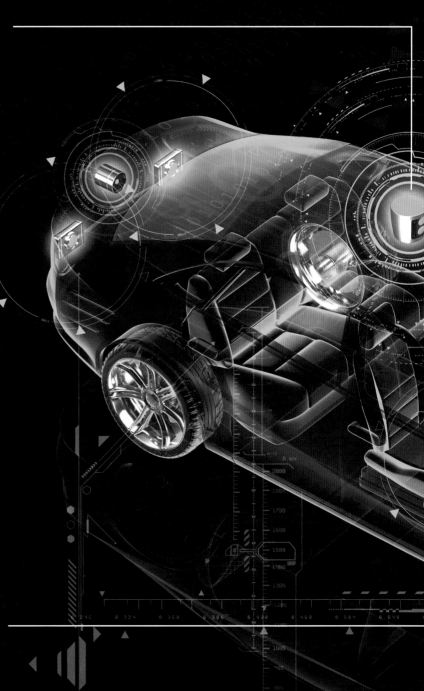

Cameras. Cameras take in visible light. Multiple cameras at different points around the car can be used to tell how far away objects are, just as people can do with two eyes. They are also good at recognizing moving objects. Cameras are crucial for detecting road signs and signals: a radar or lidar might detect a square sign, but only a camera could see that it says, "DO NOT ENTER."

Redesigned cabin (future). When people are not needed to drive the car in any way and self-driving cars are specially designed from the ground up, new forms will emerge. The steering wheel, mirrors, and other driving control areas will be removed. Seats may face each other, enabling people to comfortably hold conversations or play games.

Artificial intelligence. Computer learning will play a big part in the self-driving car revolution. You know what a stop sign looks like—and what you're supposed to do when you reach one. But this isn't second nature for a self-driving car. It will have many thousands of pictures of stop signs stored in its memory. It will compare objects it encounters along its journey with these images to determine if it should stop.

345:

575

694

BLAST FROM THE PAST

It may be hard to imagine life without cars and trucks. But just a little over 100 years ago, cars and trucks didn't even exist. Rich people and goods were carted about in horse-drawn carriages. But most people walked wherever they needed to go. Few people traveled more than a few dozen miles or kilometers from their homes during their whole lives.

When automobiles were a new invention, horses sharing the road had to be introduced and become accustomed to their mechanical replacements.

Who invented the car? The automobile has no single inventor. Many people worked on powered vehicles since the beginning of the Industrial Revolution. The first powered land vehicles used steam power. Then, battery-powered automobiles took over, but these were quickly replaced by cars with internal combustion engines.

Cars: the green alternative? It's hard to believe today, but cars were put forth as an environmentally friendly alternative to horses! In large cities, horses took up lots of space and ate lots of food. Worse, their manure covered city streets, making them unwalkable. "Horseless carriages" were a solution to the horse problem. Only later did people realize that these devices could themselves contribute to such other problems, as smog, accidents, congestion, and global warming.

PERFECTLY SIMPLE - SIMPLY PERFECT

"Maxwell"
Model G A Roadster
4 cylinder, 30 H.P. $1600

A woman uses a hand-cranked battery charger to recharge her electric automobile in 1912. Early electric cars required frequent recharging.

Electric cars aren't as futuristic as they seem. Some of the first automobiles were powered with batteries. But they were slow, heavy, and had very short ranges. In 1908, the American automobile company Ford released the gasoline-powered Model T. The Model T was cheap, reliable, easy to repair, and had a long range. Electric cars quickly disappeared from the market for some 100 years until improvements in battery technology and concerns about greenhouse gas emissions led to their modern revival.

THE BUMPY ROAD TO SELF-DRIVING CARS

Not long after cars were developed, the freedom they gave their drivers to go anywhere turned into a curse, as more and more motorists crammed into gridlocked road systems. With the rise of computers, people reasoned that the drudgery of the commute could be done away with if cars could drive themselves. But this dream has proven harder to achieve than first thought.

592   *Radio News for November, 1925*

Radio-Controlled Automobile
By HERNDON GREEN

Radio is to control a car in transcontinental tour. The system, which is extremely simple and effective, is fully described here.

...RAM

...diagram given in
...on will show the
...n. Some of the
...out in order to

...e of the usual
...battery supply

LE PETIT JOURNAL
ILLUSTRÉ

UNE AUTO SANS CONDUCTEUR SE PROMÈNE DANS PARIS

The phantom auto. In 1925, the Houdina Company created a car that cruised around New York City with no driver at the wheel *(above),* startling and amazing onlookers. But Houdina was a remote-control company, not a self-driving car company—the car was driven by a person nearby. The gimmick however, got people thinking about how to make the trick a reality. Another "driverless" car caused a commotion on the streets of Paris *(right).*

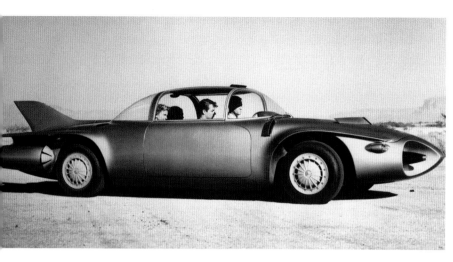

The road not taken. In 1956, GM thought the future of self-driving vehicles lay under the road. Its Firebird concept was designed to follow buried wires under the roadway. **Engineers** at GM envisioned hands-free driving in the express lanes of major highways.

The 1961 Ford Gyron *(below)* was a futuristic concept car. Ford boasted that it would have amazing capabilities—including computer-controlled navigation—but a working model was never built.

DARPA GRAND CHALLENGES

The concept of self-driving cars mostly languished as a fringe idea until the early 2000's. The Defense Advanced Research Projects Agency (DARPA), a United States government organization that works to create and use new technology, wanted to make U.S. military vehicles **autonomous.** They wanted to protect soldiers and military personnel from **improvised explosive devices** (IED's), which were plaguing convoys in Iraq and Afghanistan. But no major companies were developing autonomous vehicles at the time. So in 2004, DARPA organized a public, off-road, self-driving car race called the Grand Challenge.

Fifteen teams of robotics hobbyists, automotive engineers, and even a high school student built self-driving vehicles for the competition. The vehicles were as diverse as the teams themselves: the smallest was a self-balancing dirtbike, the largest was a modified military cargo truck. The team whose vehicle first completed the grueling, 142-mile desert course within the 10-hour time limit was to receive $1 million.

The prize money went unclaimed. The self-balancing dirtbike flipped over at the starting line. The military truck got stuck between two wispy tumbleweeds, perceiving them to be solid objects. Another truck traveled 20 feet (6 meters) before turning around and returning to the starting line. The best vehicle traveled only 7.5 (12 kilomerers) miles before veering off course and getting stuck in a ditch.

Though no vehicle finished the course, the contest was spectacular. DARPA imme-

diately announced a second competition for the following year and doubled the prize. This time, several teams completed the race. Another urban-themed challenge followed in 2007. Many of the people who participated in these challenges went on to become major figures in the self-driving car industry.

Many of the entries for the DARPA Challenge were built from modified versions of typical vehicles. The AVIDOR 2004 (above) was basically a modified dunebuggy.

VELODYNE ACOUSTICS

David Hall headed a speaker company called Velodyne Acoustics. In the early 2000's, with his company struggling, Hall experimented with self-driving car technology and bet that lidar would be a crucial sensor component. He thought that if the laser array spun, it could take in the whole environment at once. He and his brother entered the 2004 Grand Challenge. They didn't win, of course, but DARPA officials—as well as other contestants—immediately saw the value of his design. Today, Velodyne is the top lidar manufacturer in the world.

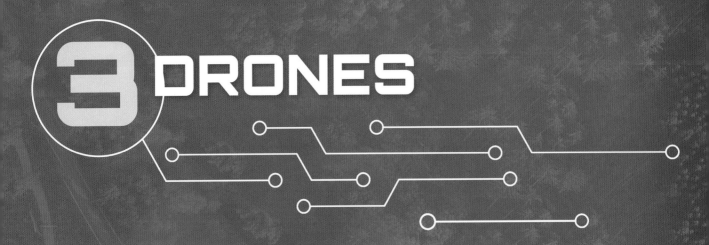

3 DRONES

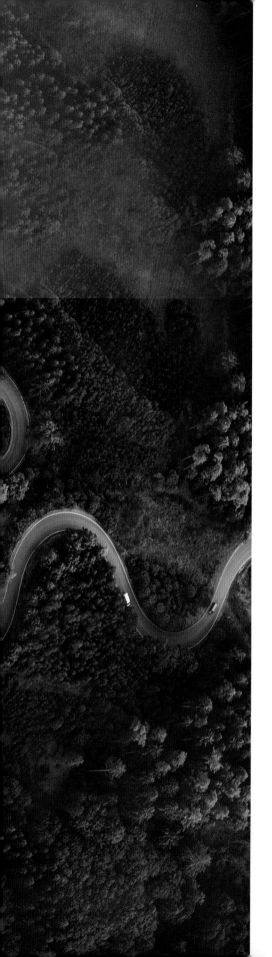

LOOK! UP IN THE SKY! IT'S A BIRD! IT'S A PLANE! IT'S A DRONE!

Maybe you have a **drone.** You might race it around trees and poles, do stunts, or capture amazing aerial video. Apart from being cool toys, *multirotor* drones (drones that have multiple—usually four or more—propellers) do some important jobs. Some capture pictures and video for television, film, and advertisements. Others have more dramatic missions, such as spying on enemies in military operations. Drones are called uncrewed aerial vehicles (UAV's). That's technically true, because there is no crew on board. But almost all drones are piloted by a person on the ground.

Multirotor drones have been limited to aerial photography because they are relative weaklings. Such drones use electric motors and rotors to take off and land vertically. Their batteries can't hold as much energy as the same amount of gasoline or jet fuel. But their electric motors make them cheap, quiet, and easy to maintain. As engineers create better batteries, multirotor drones will be able to do more and more things.

Imagine buying an item online in the morning and having it waiting at your door by lunchtime. With flying delivery drones, almost every item under a few pounds or kilograms could be delivered in minutes. In addition to being more convenient, delivery drones could help cut traffic congestion. Trucks represent 7% of traffic on city roads, but they account for 18% of the congestion costs of cities, measured by wasted fuel and time. Replacing slow-moving trucks with delivery drones could save money for delivery companies and save time for commuters.

Future drones may also help find people in disasters and drop supplies to them. In developing countries or those affected by war, drones could safely deliver food, medicine, or other supplies to people who need it.

HOW DRONES WORK

Multirotor drones didn't become popular thanks to some flashy prototype or a break-through innovation. Instead, they have been propelled by improvements to some relatively mundane technologies. It's not exciting news if engineers create an electric motor that's a little bit more reliable, or a battery that can store a little more energy. But such everyday engineering has made multirotor drones possible. Today, most of these drones are cool toys. But they'll soon be used for all kinds of commercial applications.

Batteries. Powerful rechargeable batteries have enabled drones to go electric. A battery has no moving parts, unlike gasoline-burning engines, so a battery-powered drone needs much less maintenance and repair.

Cameras. Advances in camera systems have made drones both easier to fly and more useful. A screen can be embedded in the pilot's controls, allowing him or her to see what the drone sees. Advanced cameras paired with computer systems enable some drones to fly autonomously.

Motors. The development of cheap, powerful, reliable electric motors has allowed engineers to design drones with multiple rotors. Because the forces from multiple rotors balance each other out, there is no need for a tail rotor like the one found in most helicopters. If one (or in some cases, even more) of a drone's rotors or motors fails, it can steady itself and perform a controlled emergency landing. Also, a multirotor drone can be steered simply by adjusting the speeds of the motors. A helicopter needs a complex mechanism called a swashplate to adjust its main rotor in order to steer.

RADIO CONTROL

As some inventors were experimenting with powered flight, others were experimenting with remote control. In an 1898 demonstration in New York City, the inventor Nikola Tesla stunned onlookers by piloting a large toy boat from several feet (a few meters) away. At the time, few people knew about **radio waves,** so the thought of commanding a device without any wires seemed like magic. In fact, the technology was so ahead of its time that Tesla couldn't convince anyone of its usefulness. It took almost 20 years before the U.S. military started experimenting with remote control.

Remote control. Almost all multirotor drones today are piloted by someone on the ground via remote control. Even if future drones are more autonomous, they might still have radio communication abilities to receive emergency commands and to communicate with other drones.

DELIVERY DRONES

As drones become more powerful, many people imagine them carrying more than just cameras and sensors. Several companies are investing in a future where drones deliver products to people.

Amazon. The company Amazon is the most famous company pursuing drone technology. In 2016, it used an autonomous drone to make a delivery in the United Kingdom. This was just a trial, but Amazon is hoping to scale up its efforts soon. It has put forth all kinds of ideas in **patents,** including giant, flying, blimp-like warehouses where drones can get merchandise and recharge!

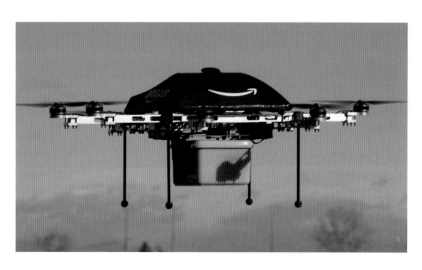

Zipline. A company called Zipline is already using drones to make deliveries of blood to hospitals and clinics in Rwanda, a small country in east-central Africa. Rwanda has an unreliable road network. It takes many hours to transport blood to rural clinics. Zipline's drone can deliver blood to participating locations in less than 30 minutes. The airplane-like drone is loaded and launched from Zipline's base, flies autonomously to the drop point, and releases its cargo from the air. The container filled with individually packed units of blood parachutes to the clinic, and the drone flies back to its base.

Delivery drones are perfect for sending small and lighter packages short distances. Drones could replace many deliveries currently made by road-clogging trucks.

Legal concerns. Governments are concerned that drones be used safely. In the United States, drones must never leave the sight of their pilot (or their emergency pilot, if they're autonomous). They must also avoid flying over people and cars. These laws are big roadblocks to the expansion of drone usage, but they were put in place to keep people safe. As companies show that they can operate drones safely under a variety of conditions, these laws will probably be relaxed.

TACOCOPTER

In the mood for tacos? Call Tacocopter! In 2012, a website was launched promising drone-delivered tacos in the San Francisco area. But after attracting media attention, it was revealed to be a hoax.

4 PASSENGER DRONES

THE FLYING CAR REINVENTED

Conventional flying cars will probably never achieve widespread popularity. There are too many hurdles to creating an inexpensive vehicle that can both fly and drive safely. But what if you combine the strategies being developed by self-driving car companies with drone technology, and do away with the wheels entirely? Think of a delivery drone: it will autonomously deliver packages. Now, imagine scaling up a delivery drone to create a short-range aircraft that can autonomously shuttle people to their destinations—no pilot's license required!

Passenger drones would completely transform urban transportation, from the dense downtown to the sleepy suburbs. Residents farther from the city center might walk or take a self-driving shuttle to a neighborhood drone port. From there, they could fly to anywhere in the city within a half-hour. There would be no reason for skyscrapers to have one entry at ground level. Many tall buildings might have a droneport on their roof. Supertall skyscrapers might even have droneports at different levels, so people could be dropped off closer to their destination.

With an efficient air-traffic control system, people could move around with ease in passenger drones. Drones would probably fly along designated routes, like highways in the sky. But these skyways would be far more flexible than roads. If many drones indicate to the air-traffic control system that they are going to the same destination—such as to or from a concert—the system might plan an "expressway" to take them all there from the city center.

City streets used to be public spaces where vendors sold goods, couples strolled, and children played. In the last century, cars and traffic changed all that. But with widespread use of passenger and delivery drones, many streets may once again be turned over to people, becoming marketplaces, parkland, and bike paths.

HOW PASSENGER DRONES WILL WORK

A passenger drone looks a lot different than your stereotypical flying car. Gone are the cumbersome wings, funky wheels, and noisy engines. In their place is an elegant cabin, quiet propellers, and efficient battery packs.

Power. Most passenger drone inventors envision them being battery powered. Despite major improvements in battery technology over the decades, they are not yet powerful enough to allow for flights of more than a half-hour or so. A few companies are experimenting with **hybrid** drives, where a small gasoline engine is used to recharge the craft's batteries. Either way, passenger drones' fuel efficiency will set them apart from helicopters, which usually have jet engines that burn lots of fuel.

Autonomy. Helicopters are hard to control, even for experienced pilots. Multirotor drones are similar. Given the populous environments passenger drones would fly in, they would likely be completely autonomous. Everyone could relax and enjoy the view while they are ferried to their destination. An autonomous system would ensure that the craft stays in the appropriate airspace and doesn't collide with buildings, birds, or other drones as it travels to its destination.

Multiple motors and rotors. Most of these craft have multiple rotors. This eliminates the need for the tail rotor found in traditional helicopters. Redundancy ensures the vehicle is able to make a safe landing even in the case of multiple failures—just like a traditional drone. As a last resort, many designs include an emergency whole-vehicle parachute.

One day soon, the sky may be full of passenger drones like these. Designs for passenger drones vary according to their range and how many passengers can be carried.

5 JETPACKS

Like a modern-day Icarus, humans have always dreamt of having wings and taking flight. Cool new technologies are set to make personal jetpacks a reality.

THE QUINTESSENTIAL FUTURISTIC INVENTION

What could be cooler than strapping on a jetpack and speeding through the air? Just like the flying car, the jetpack is the poster-invention for the future that never arrived. That future has, in fact, arrived, just not quite on the scale that everyone hoped.

Bell Rocket Belt. The first jetpack, the Small Rocket Lift Device *(left),* was successfully tested in 1960. The pack used tiny rocket engines that were fueled by hydrogen peroxide (H_2O_2), rather than jet engines. It could lift its pilot for only about 20 seconds, far too short of a time to propel soldiers into or out of combat.

Hiller Flying Platform. The Hiller Flying Platform *(right)* was developed in the 1950's. It had two shielded rotors positioned under the pilot's feet. The pilot leaned to steer the craft. The design was interesting, but it couldn't meet the military's requirements of speed and redundancy.

JETPACKS HERE AND NOW

Today, jetpacks exist in all shapes and sizes. They're either in development or extremely expensive. But you might be able to use one on your next vacation!

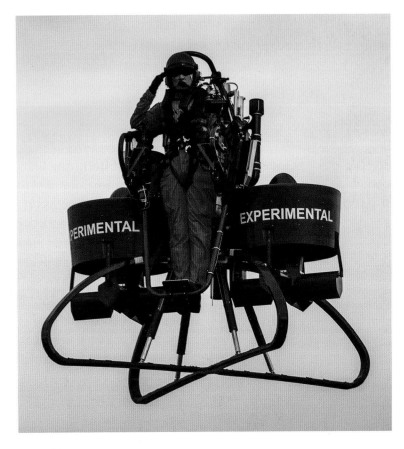

Fanpack? Similar to the Hiller Flying Platform, the Martin Jetpack uses two ducted fans to propel its pilot into the air. In addition to its traditional mode, the vehicle will be able to be piloted remotely or autonomously follow a person or another jetpack to ferry supplies into rough terrain.

Water jetpacks. Several companies make recreational water jetpacks. These devices shoot streams of water at high speed to keep the pilot aloft. People can fly around and perform tricks on these craft. But they need a constant supply of high-pressure water, so they have to connect to a personal watercraft with a long hose. Therefore, they can only fly over water.

Jet jetpack. Perhaps the coolest jetpacks are the models from Jetpack Aviation, which use actual jet engines. The jetpacks' long range and high lift capacities have attracted much interest, including, again, from the military. But the company is hesitant to sell until it has perfected pilot safety.

THE INCREDIBLE IRON MAN

In the comic book and movie franchise *Iron Man*, billionaire inventor Tony Stark develops a suit that gives him the ability to fly. Unfortunately, his suit relies on futuristic technology that won't be developed for many years—if at all.

6 SUPERSONIC PASSENGER PLANES

FASTER THAN SOUND

Today, no passenger airplane goes faster than 760 miles (1,220 kilometers) per hour. That's pretty fast, but Earth is a big place: going that speed, it takes 20 or more hours to travel halfway across the globe—so long, in fact, that the commercial airliners capable of making such a flight nonstop are only now just being developed. Why are jetliners limited to this speed?

Breaking the sound barrier. 760 miles per hour is the speed that sound waves travel through the air. Before 1947, people thought that sustained flight faster than sound wasn't possible. Most experts thought the shock would break the plane apart. It was called the sound barrier—an invisible wall in the air. But on October 14 of that year, U.S. test pilot Chuck Yeager broke through the barrier while piloting the specially designed Bell X-1 rocket plane. Yeager reported no ill effects to himself or the aircraft—in fact, he expressed disappointment at how uneventful the crossing was! Encouraged by the results, engineers quickly designed many supersonic (faster than sound) planes for the military.

Speedy advances, speedy travel. During the 1950's, people in the United States benefited from military technology developed during World War II, (1939-1945). **Mass production** made cars affordable to many people. Air travel was becoming ever cheaper and faster. The first passenger planes were propeller-driven craft that could only fly a few hundred miles per hour. But in 1952, the first jetliner, the De Havilland Comet, debuted, capable of speeds of 500 miles per hour. With the highly publicized flight of the Bell X-1, many people believed supersonic passenger jets were only a few years away.

THE RISE AND FALL OF CONCORDE

Wait—wasn't there already a supersonic passenger plane? Although planes can fly faster than the speed of sound, it's been hard to make supersonic passenger planes profitable. One supersonic airplane flew commercial routes for 27 years, but none do today.

In the 1960's, the United States, the Soviet Union (a country made up of what is now Russia and surrounding European and Asian countries), and a joint partnership between the United Kingdom and France raced to develop the first supersonic passenger jets. The U.S. got a late start and eventually dropped out of the race. The Soviet Union completed their jet first, but it was uncomfortable and dangerous. The U.K.-France partnership produced a plane called Concorde, which made its first supersonic test flight in 1969. It was an elegant plane, but it was expensive, high-maintenance, and—to people on the ground—loud.

Like all supersonic planes, Concorde produced a sonic boom when it broke the sound barrier. This loud noise startled people and animals and could even shatter windows if the plane was close enough

to the ground. In 1973, the United States banned nonmilitary supersonic flight over land, severely limiting Concorde's market. European countries quickly followed suit. Concorde's flights, which began in 1976, were limited to routes across the Atlantic Ocean. The two airlines that used it, British Airways and Air France, carved out a small market flying wealthy tourists and business travelers from Paris or London to New York in less than three and a half hours. But the planes guzzled fuel and were expensive to maintain, so, the airlines struggled to keep the service profitable.

In 2000, a Concorde crashed in France during take-off, killing all 109 people on board and 4 on the ground. Investigators later found that debris on the runway caused the crash. But the planes were grounded for a year while the investigations took place, and Concorde's reputation never recovered. In 2003, both British Airways and Air France ended their Concorde flights. There hasn't been a supersonic passenger plane since.

THE SOVIET TUPELOV

The Soviet Tupolev Tu-144 actually beat Concorde to supersonic flight by a matter of months. But the plane was inefficient, noisy, and dangerous. It suffered from two deadly crashes during testing, which delayed its commercial rollout until after Concorde's. It was so loud in the cabin that passengers couldn't talk to each other and had to pass around notes to communicate. The Tu-144 flew just one flight a week for less than a year before it was permanently grounded.

CAN SUPERSONIC PASSENGER PLANES FLY AGAIN?

It may seem that supersonic flight was a failed experiment in the field of transportation. But it might be staging a comeback. Changing economics, combined with smart engineering decisions, may make supersonic jetliners viable again. Then you might be able to take a quick weekend trip to another continent!

Lowering the boom. Noise from sonic booms can actually be reduced with careful engineering. Using **computer-aided design,** engineers are studying how different wing shapes and engine placements affect the volume of a sonic boom. The companies that are designing new supersonic passenger planes are working to convince governments that their planes will be quiet enough to fly over land. In the meantime, they are planning to serve transoceanic routes, where there are no supersonic restrictions.

Economy of speed. The new supersonic jet companies are trying to sell their speed as an economic advantage to airlines. Since a supersonic jet could make a transatlantic crossing about twice as fast as a traditional commercial plane, a supersonic jet could theoretically fly twice as many routes, carrying twice as many paying passengers as a similarly-sized conventional plane. But this will only work if the tickets are priced high enough to make up for the increased fuel use, demand is high enough to fill the flights, and maintenance is simple enough to keep the planes in the air.

> The Lockheed Martin X-plane *(below)* is one of the new low boom supersonic aircraft designs. The Aerion AS2 *(right)* can cruise faster than any jet today without the sonic boom.

7 HYPERLOOPS

BEYOND TRAINS

Say you're going to the next big city over—some 200 to 300 miles (300 to 500 kilometers) away—to visit a friend. How do you get there? For many, this scenario is the transportation twilight zone. A flight would require traveling to an airport, checking in, going through security, and enduring inevitable delays, all for a maddeningly short flight. Driving promises many uncomfortable, grueling hours on the road.

Trains are an option for some trips, but they can be even slower than driving in the United States. Train tracks are mostly built at ground level, so passenger trains have to contend with track obstructions and slow down at road crossings. They also have to share the tracks with slow-moving freight trains.

Even once they get rolling, fast-moving trains face several challenges. Friction between the wheels and tracks, called rolling resistance, slows the train. Due to the way train wheels are designed, trains can wobble and derail at extreme speeds, even on straight track. The faster a train travels, the greater the effect of air resistance, especially in tunnels. The train has to push air out of its way, wasting energy.

A concept called the hyperloop hopes to solve these challenges and revolutionize mid-range travel. Imagine going the speed of a passenger jet just above the ground, but with fewer of the complicated logistics and less of the waiting periods of air travel. Using special cars and tubes, passengers and freight could travel at speeds of over 700 miles (1,100 kilometers) per hour. The financial hurdles to constructing such a network are huge, but several companies are working to make this dream a reality.

HOW HYPERLOOPS WILL WORK

Research into Goddard's vactrains (see page 45) was kickstarted by another rock-etry pioneer more than 100 years later. In a 2013 paper, South African-born entre-preneur Elon Musk described a system much like the vactrain that could transport people and freight at high speeds through tubes. He called the system a hyperloop. Musk, then a CEO of two separate companies, declined to pursue the technology himself. But his company SpaceX frequently hosts hyperloop design competitions.

Evacuated tube. At high speeds, air resistance slows down a moving object. Hyperloop tubes would have most of the air removed by pumps placed along the track. A compressor might also be included in the vehicle to take in any leftover air in front of it and push it out the back. Combined with magnetic levitation, evacuated tubes would allow the pods to accelerate and cruise us-ing very little energy. The tubes will likely be elevated or buried underground so other kinds of traffic don't get in the way.

Linear induction motors. Linear induction motors (LIM's) built into the tube itself will pull and push the pod along. Placing the LIM's along the tube makes the pods simpler and sets "speed limits" for each section of track. Pods would automatically cruise at the speed which the closest LIM's have been programmed with.

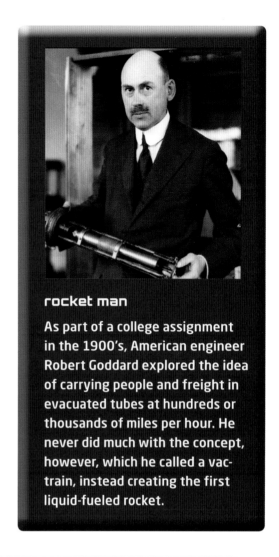

rocket man

As part of a college assignment in the 1900's, American engineer Robert Goddard explored the idea of carrying people and freight in evacuated tubes at hundreds or thousands of miles per hour. He never did much with the concept, however, which he called a vac-train, instead creating the first liquid-fueled rocket.

Magnetic levitation. Think about trying to push two magnets together. If you replace the wheels and tracks of a train with strong magnets, the whole train can float, losing no energy to friction. Some slower, small-scale maglev (short for magnetic levitation) trains exist. A high-speed model is being tested in Japan that can exceed 370 miles (600 kilometers) per hour. In a hyperloop, pods would float through the tube using magnetic levitation. This would eliminate rolling resistance and the danger of derailing.

GLOSSARY

autonomous capable of acting independently.

computer-aided design (CAD) the use of computers to design manufactured objects.

drone an uncrewed aerial vehicle. Most drones are piloted remotely, but some are autonomous.

ducted propeller a propeller that turns within a cylindrical device called a duct.

engineer a professional who plans and builds engines, machines, roads, or the like.

fuselage the body of an airplane, helicopter, or glider to which the wings, tail, and other parts are fastened.

Global Positioning System (GPS) a worldwide navigation system that uses radio signals broadcast by satellites.

hybrid combining two or more functions or modes of operation.

improvised explosive device (IED) a bomb that is homemade or otherwise put together by an amateur.

infrared rays light that has wavelengths longer than those of the red part of the visible spectrum and shorter than those of microwaves.

laser a device that produces a very narrow and intense beam of a very narrow range of light wavelengths going in only one direction. By contrast, a standard light source produces light of many wavelengths all traveling in slightly different directions.

lidar a sensing method in which pulses of laser light are used to measure distances and create three-dimensional pictures of an environment.

lift the upward reaction of an aircraft into an area of less dense air flowing over its airfoil, such as a wing or rotor blade.

linear induction motor an electric motor that produces linear thrust directly with the push or pull of magnetic fields rather than by rotation.

mass production the creation of machinery and other articles in standard sizes in large numbers.

patent a government grant which gives a person or company sole rights to make, use, or sell, a new invention for a certain number of years.

resolution the ability of a lens or sensor to produce separate images of objects that are very close together.

sensor a device that takes in information from the outside world and translates it into code.

INDEX

A

accidents: car, 8, 13; plane, 39
Aerion AS2 plane, 40-41
Air France, 39
airplanes, 8, 10; supersonic, 35-41
Amazon (company), 26
artificial intelligence, 13, 15
automobiles. *See* cars
autonomous systems, 24, 26, 29, 30. *See also* self-driving cars
Autoplane, 10
AVIDOR 2004 (vehicle), 21

B

batteries, 16, 17, 23, 24, 30
Bell X-1 rocket plane, 37
British Airways, 39

C

cameras, 15, 24
cars, 5, 10; early, 8, 16-17; electric, 16, 17. *See also* flying cars; self-driving cars
Concorde supersonic plane, 38-39
Curtiss, Glenn, 10

D

Defense Advanced Research Project Agency (DARPA), 20-21
De Havilland Comet (jetliner), 37
drones: delivery, 26-27, 29; multirotor, 22-27, 30-31; passenger, 28-31

E

electric cars, 16, 17

F

Firebird (car), 19
flying cars, 6-11; drones as, 29; early, 8-10
Ford Motor Company, 17, 19

G

General Motors (GM), 19
Global Positioning System (GPS), 14
Goddard, Robert, 44, 45
Grand Challenges, 20-21
Gyron (car), 19

H

Hall, David, 21
helicopters, 30
Hiller Flying Platform, 33
horses, 16
Houdina Company, 18
hyperloops, 42-45

I

Iron Man (movie), 35

J

jetliners, 5, 37
Jetpack Aviation (company), 35
jetpacks, 32-37

L

lidar, 14, 21
linear induction motors (LIM's), 45
Lockheed Martin X-plane, 40

M

magnetic levitation, 44, 45
Martin jetpack, 34
Model T, 17
motors: car, 16, 17; drone, 23, 25, 30; hyperloop, 45
Musk, Elon, 44

P

propellers, ducted, 9, 11

R

radar, 14
remote control, 23, 25
rockets, 33, 45
rolling resistance, 43

rotors, 33, 34. *See also* drones
Rwanda, 26

S

self-driving cars, 12-21; early, 18-19; parts of, 14-15; program for developing, 20-21
Small Rocket Lift Device, 33
sonic booms, 38, 40
sound barrier, 37, 38
Soviet Union, 38, 39
supersonic passenger planes, 36-41

T

Tacocopter hoax, 27
Taylor Aerocar, 9
Tesla (company), 14
Tesla, Nikola, 25
traffic congestion, 7, 13, 18, 23, 29
trains, 43
transportation, 5
Tupelov Tu-144 plane, 39

U

uncrewed aerial vehicles (UAV's), 23

V

vactrains, 44, 45
Velodyne Acoustics, 21

W

water jetpacks, 34
wings, flying car, 8-11

Y

Yeager, Chuck, 37

Z

Zipline (company), 26

ACKNOWLEDGMENTS

5   © Chesky/Shutterstock

6-7 © Terrafugia; © Mike Dotta, Shutterstock

8-9 © macchina Volantis; © Museum of Flight Foundation/Getty Images

10-11 © Archivist/Adobe Stock; © Terrafugia; © Urban Aeronautics

12-13 © Daimler AG; © VCG/Getty Images

14-15 © Ikon Images/Masterfile; © Chesky/Shutterstock

16-17 Public Domain; Library of Congress; © Stock Montage/Getty Images; © Schenectady Museum/Getty Images

18-19 Public Domain; © Leemage/UIG/Getty Images; © Bettmann/Getty Images; © GraphicaArtis/Getty Images

20-21 DARPA; © Vaughn Youtz, ZUMA Press/Alamy Images; Image courtesy of David Hall; © Velodyne Lidar

22-23 © Rocksweeper/Shutterstock

24-25 © Dmitry Kalinovsky, Shutterstock; © Motorama/Shutterstock; © Dorde/Shutterstock

26-27 © Amazon; © Zipline; © Maroke/Shutterstock; WOLRD BOOK photo by Don Di Sante; © Kaleo/Shutterstock

28-29 © U3D/Shutterstock

30-31 © Andrey I/Shutterstock; © Chesky/Shutterstock; © Dolorean Aerospace

32-33 © Fabrice Coffrini, AFP/Getty Images; © Ed Clark, The LIFE Picture Collection/Getty Images; © Getty Images

34-35 © Martin Jetpack; © Chuck Wagner, Shutterstock; © JetPack Aviation; © Paramount Pictures

36-37 © Aerion Supersonic; NASA; © Museum of Flight/Getty Images

38-39 © Agsaz/Shutterstock; © Manchester Daily Express/Getty Images; © Keystone-France/Getty Images

40-41 NASA/Lockheed Martin; © Aerion Supersonic

42-43 © Hyperloop One

44-45 © Hyperloop One; © Bettmann/Getty Images; © Andrey I/Shutterstock

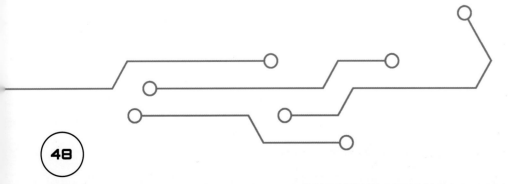